Magnetic Race Car

written by Anne Giulieri

photography by Ned Meldrum

hinkler

Engage Literacy
published by Hinkler Education
a division of Hinkler Books Pty Ltd
45–55 Fairchild Street
Heatherton Victoria 3202 Australia
www.hinklereducation.com.au

First published in 2012
10 9 8 7 6 5 4 3 2 1

Written by Anne Giulieri
Lead authors Jay Dale and Anne Giulieri
Photography by Ned Meldrum
Edited by Gwenda Smyth
Designed by Susannah Low, Butterflyrocket Design

Magnetic Race Car
ISBN: 978 1 7428 1153 6

Acknowledgments
p5 bottom center: Shutterstock.com/ © nikkytok; p7 top: © Yongong | Dreamstime.com; p7 bottom: © Natursports | Dreamstime.com;

Table of Contents

Materials

Here are all the materials you will need to make a magnetic race car and its *racetrack*.

tape
horseshoe magnet
CARNIVAL Arts & Crafts
HOBBY PVA Glue
NON STAINING
DRIES CLEAR
NON TOXIC
60 mL
strong glue
buttons
colored paper
string
crayons, markers, or colored pencils
LARGE CRAYONS

The first thing you need to do is collect the materials you will need. You will need a very small box—an old matchbox is ideal.

You might like to search for ideas on how to *decorate* the box to make it look like a real race car. You could look at books or search the Internet on a computer.

Making the Race Car

After you have gathered some ideas, decorate your small box so that it looks like a race car. You could cover it in white paper and then decorate it with crayons, markers, or colored pencils.

Drawing stripes down the side of your box just like a real race car is a good idea, too.

Small wheels can be attached to the box. You can make four small wheels by cutting them out of paper and attaching them to the box. Or you could use some old buttons, and stick these on with some strong glue. You could even place a race car number on each side of the box.

If you decide to put a driver in the car, you might need to make a hole in the box.

Your driver could be made from playdough or colored paper.

Once your race car is finished, attach a *magnet* underneath the car using strong glue. Make sure that you attach the magnet to the middle.

Making the Racetrack

The next thing you need to do is to prepare your racetrack for racing. This can be done by getting a large cardboard box and cutting a round hole in the side of the box. The hole must be large enough for your hand to go through. After the hand hole has been made, you can start on the racetrack.

To make the racetrack, turn the box upside down so that the opening of the box is facing downward. Find enough white paper to cover the bottom of the box. If you need to, cut the white paper so it will fit. This is where you will draw your racetrack. It is a lot easier to draw on white paper than on cardboard and your picture will stand out more.

Before gluing the paper to the box, carefully draw a racetrack around the outside of the paper. You can make the track *wind* around—just like a real racetrack. Make sure that the racetrack is *wide* enough for your race car. Be sure to draw a start and a finish line. After you have colored in the racetrack, decorate the *surrounding* area. It is your decision how you decorate it. You could color in the *remaining* area so that it looks like grass.

When you have finished decorating the white paper, glue it onto the box.

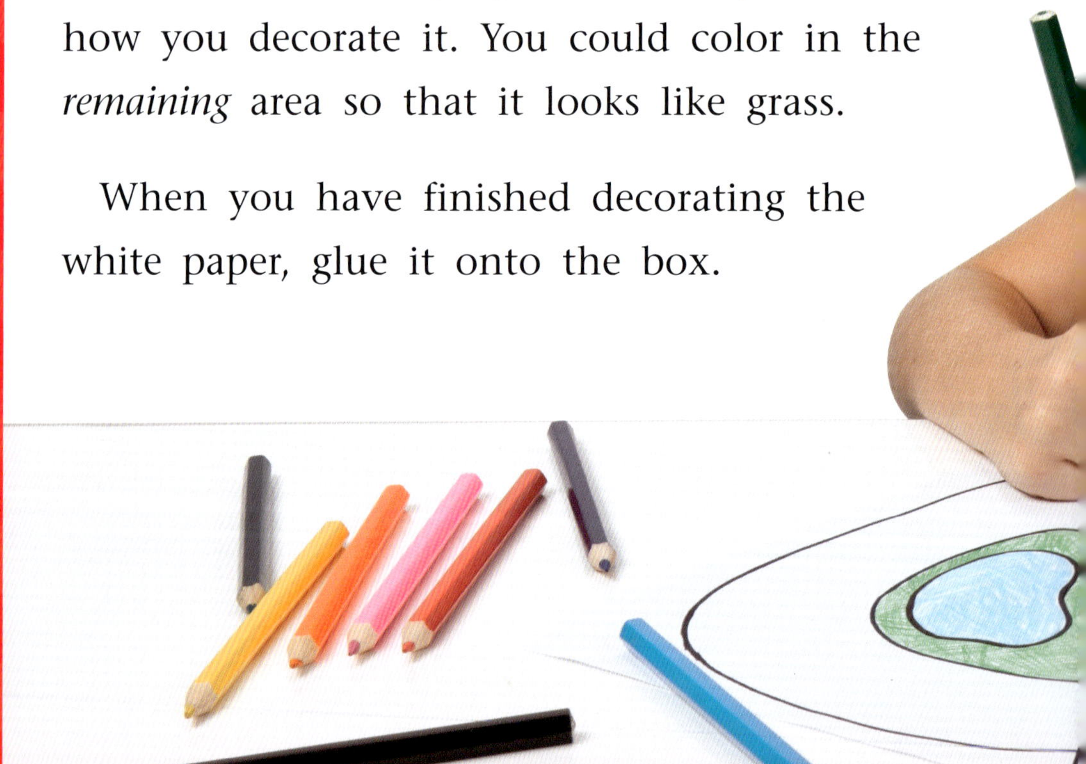

Racing Your Car

The next step is to cut a piece of string. It should be long enough to reach all corners of your box. Tape one end of the string inside the box, below the round hole.

Pick up the horseshoe magnet.

DID YOU KNOW?

It is called a horseshoe magnet because it is shaped like the shoe of a horse.

Now *tie* the other end of the string around the horseshoe magnet, so that you don't lose this important piece of *equipment*. Carefully place the box on the table or ground with the racetrack facing up.

Place your car on the racetrack at the starting line. Then, while holding the horseshoe magnet, put your hand through the hole. Hold the horseshoe magnet under your racetrack, just beneath your car. Make sure the open end of the magnet is touching the box.

Finally, you are ready to race! As you carefully move the horseshoe magnet you will be amazed to see your race car move, too! As you *guide* your race car along the track, try to keep your hand steady. That way the horseshoe magnet will stay under the track.

See if you can "drive" your race car all the way around the racetrack. Each time you do it, you will improve.

Glossary

decorate: add things to an object to make it look better

equipment: things you need in order to do a task

guide: help to move in the correct direction

magnet: something made of metal that attracts other metals

racetrack: a special road for cars, bikes or people to use when racing

remaining: left over

surrounding: outside, around or nearby

tie: attach with thread, string or rope

wide: big from side to side

wind (wind around): turn and twist

Index